LIVING WITH & LOVING ALL of GOD'S CHILDREN-
A Primer for Youth-
Musings on manners and more...

Ronald H. Bartalini

Sundie Enterprises
Since 1972

Copyright © 2016 by Ronald H. Bartalini
All rights reserved.

In accordance with the U.S. Copyright act of 1976, the scanning, uploading, and electronic sharing of any part of this book without the permission of the publisher is unlawful piracy and theft of the author's intellectual property. If you would like to use material from the book (other than for review purposes), prior written permission must be obtained from the publisher at permission:

Sundie Enterprises
P.O. Box 1274
Provo, Utah 84603-1274

ISBN 978-0-9859811-5-0
Library of Congress Card Catalogue Number:
2015919612
Bartalini, Ron

Description: This book will show you how to better live with and love all of God's children. In it, you will learn about manners, social interaction, and much more. Just begin turning the pages, and you will discover that loving all of God's children can be fun!

Dedication

For *all of God's children*

Appreciation

My heartfelt thanks goes to my neighbor and friend, Bill Baker who volunteered to be my editor. The title of this book came from him.

The book you are about to read began as the first part of *"Change For the Better Forever."* When Bill and I sat down to read the contents we soon realized I had two books instead of one. As I continued my work on *"Change For the Better Forever"* it has evolved into four books: *"Living With and Loving All of God's Children-A Primer for Youth-Musings on Manners and More," "Growing Up In America- A Primer for Youth-Musings on Making Your Dreams Come True and More." "The Power of Forgiveness,"* and finally, *"Change Your Life Forever."*

That each may be helpful in its own way. Ronald H. Bartalini, January, 2016.

Preface

God's children come in many shapes, sizes and persuasions. We are commanded to love all, and not only as we love ourselves, but unconditionally, even as our beloved Father for Christ's sake, loves all of us.

We cannot effectively love all of God's children by talking about love, or preaching a sermon on it, or writing about it. Although that is a good start, we must get out there and do something-one small act of kindness at a time.

"And the second (great commandment) is like unto it. Thou shalt love thy neighbor as thyself" (Matthew 22:39, emphasis added).
"Love one another as I have loved you" (John 15:12).

Ten Suggestions for Getting the Most Out of This Book:

A. **Decide to Change Your Life**

Did you know that making the decision to change your life for the better has the power to change your life for the better forever? If you decide now what you will not do, then when the time for making a decision comes, you will already know what you will do. You will not have to wait to think about what your decision will be. You will not have to hesitate to make a decision, you will have already made it.

B. **Visualize and Imagine...See the New You**

Do you realize and understand that everyone who has ever amounted to anything once began just like you? First they were an infant, then a child, then a young adult, before they grew into adulthood. What separates some from the rest of the crowd? Perhaps it is just this simple. Those who achieved greatness saw themselves as achieving distinction. They visualized and imagined themselves as already being the success they hoped for and that quality drove them to achieve the victory.

C. Do Not Compare Yourself to Other People

Most people will disappoint you. That is because we are not perfect Compare yourself to the great Exemplar, even Jesus Christ. He is the only perfect person to walk the earth, and he will never disappoint you. He will always be there for you, to accept you as you are, and where you are spiritually, right now. He will always be reaching out and inviting you to come and follow him. Our beloved Savior's invitation is for all: "Come unto me, all ye that labor and are heavy laden and I will give you rest." (Matthew 11:28).
Follow the example of Christ in all of your comings and goings in this life. Ask yourself, "What would Jesus do?" When you respond similarly you will do well.

D. Read This Book With Your Family or with Friends

Oftentimes when we read in isolation we can miss some meanings and implications. Reading alone is a good thing and we should never stop doing that. However, I learned long ago, that everyone I will ever meet will know at least one thing that I do not know. They will also have had experiences I have yet to have had.

E. Invite Everyone in Your Group to Take a Turn Reading One or More Sub-headings As You Desire

It may be helpful for parents and children or friends of all ages to read this book together. This could be a way for youth to acquire some adult wisdom without having to wait until you are an adult. You cannot over-estimate the value of reading together and discussing the principles being taught as a group. When you read in a group setting, you may be able to share some experiences you have already had with someone much older.

F. Discuss What Has Been Read

Even the youngest children can share their own thoughts, which can influence meaningfully.

G. Go Out and Practice the Principle(s) Being Taught. Do it. Get it Done.

We learn more by doing than by listening. It is hoped, that reading this book will cause the hearer to take action. We learn from reading the Bible that "faith without works is dead." (James 2:20). That is a true principle. But knowledge without action is also dead and profits us nothing. We must get out and do small acts of kindness and not just talk or hear about it.

H.   Don't Be Afraid to Fail

You must go out into the world and not be afraid to embarrass yourself should you make a mistake or two, as you truly try to become better at living with and loving, all of God's children.

I.   Discuss Your Victories and Successes the Next Time You Meet As a Group

I am a big fan of feedback and opinions from friends and even strangers about my creative work. Their suggestions always seem to make my work better and I am grateful for them.

J.   Repeat the Process

You may have to go back and re-visit a certain principle again and again before you are able to change your old habits. Someone has said, "It takes three weeks to form a new habit." But it can take longer to change some old habits. Don't be discouraged just keep going!

For instance, I still find myself answering folks who ask how I am doing with some form of the word, "good."

That is why I have given you one hundred and forty-four other ways to respond to those who may ask you, "How are you doing today?" You can read this book all the way through for entertainment. You can also pick it up on a flight, while waiting for a doctor or dentist's appointment, during your family vacation, while traveling in the back seat of your family car, or just while home relaxing. You can open it up and begin reading on any page. However, if you are truly serious about learning how to live with and love all of God's children, you will learn to have fun putting the principles discussed herein into practice.

When you reach the end of this book, you will discover your Captain's log. You may wish to record your victories and successes there for future reference.

Ronald H. Bartalini, January 2016.

Summary of the Above Suggestions

A. Decide to change your life.
B. Visualize and imagine…See the new you.
C. Do not compare yourself to other people.
D. Read this book with your family or with friends.
E. Invite everyone in the group to take a turn reading one or more sub-headings as you desire.
F. Discuss what has been read.
G. Go out and practice the principle (s) taught. Do it. Get it done.
H. Don't be afraid to fail.
I. Discuss your victories and successes the next time you meet as a group.
J. Repeat the process.

The Art of Greeting People

A word to all, but especially to youth:

Horrible Harry was quite contrary.
All Horrible Harry could say was: "I hates people!"
As a result of his indifference
Horrible Harry had no friends.
Horrible Harry was left alone in the end.
Cause all Horrible Harry could say was:
"I hates people!"

When you greet people be happy, be positive, be pleasant and say something such as, "Good morning, how are you on this fine day?" or "Good afternoon, how is your day going?" or "Good evening, how is life treating you these days?" Then stop. Wait for a response before you continue to speak.

But most important of all, don't be a Horrible Harry. Don't be angry, mean and mad all the time at everyone. Rather, try to learn to love all people. When a real life Horrible Harry was told, "if you can go over to the black board and write, "I will learn to love people" one hundred times, Harry responded by saying, "Not me, I hates people." His employer then said, "You're not a people person, are you Harry?"

"That is correct," said Harry, "I hates people." "The truth is Harry, most people are fun to be around." "Not for me," said Harry. "I hates people."

So don't be a Horrible Harry. Learn to love all of God's children, one step at a time, by being kind, pleasant, courteous, thoughtful and helpful. And to learn to love people, you might want to begin by learning how to interact with them.

First Say, "Excuse Me"

Should you be approaching someone from behind, or if they simply have yet to see you coming, wait to speak until you get their attention. Saying, "excuse me," will do this and also shows respect for the person with whom you may wish to speak.

Manners

I recently had the opportunity to visit Bermuda. It is a long and narrow island famous for its beautiful beaches punctuated with pink sand. The weather back home was cold, Christmas was approaching and I had escaped to warmer climes.

When I entered my hotel, the sign on the desk said, "Should the temperature drop below 70 degrees, your money cheerfully refunded."

I thought, "this is the place for me." I quickly discovered a private beach provided by my hotel and then located a local grocery store.

I eventually met a nice couple from England who wanted to visit a public beach. I asked directions from a local resident for them, but soon discovered I did not do that properly as I was mildly rebuked by the person giving assistance.

When asking directions or other kinds of help while visiting a foreign country, remember, you are now the foreigner. You are the one asking for help. Please treat local residents with consideration, and respect. Please be polite.

Example number one: "Can you tell me what bus to take to the public beach?" The first approach alone may make the local resident feel as if, his or her country is being invaded by foreign tourists who only know how to treat the locals as servants. The first example exemplifies mildly insensitive behavior, because you did not acknowledge the existence of the person to whom you were speaking first. In their possible perception, you may as well have been addressing a stop sign.

Example, number two: "Excuse me, sir or ma'am. How are you doing this morning, or, this afternoon or, this evening?" Now wait for their answer, then continue. "My friends are visiting from England, and I am visiting from America." Wait for their response. Then continue.

"Could you tell us which bus to take to the public beach?" The second example displays respectful and polite behavior.

Make Eye Contact Before You Speak

Typically, the optimal, or most preferred time to communicate is when the person with whom you wish to speak is making eye contact with you, and you with them. If you don't make this eye contact before you address someone, the person may feel devalued. Also, do not turn away after you begin talking with someone.

Similarly, it would be impolite to be shaking one person's hand while also turning to talk to another. Why bother to say hello if you don't keep eye contact while you are saying hello? This behavior may be innocent enough, but it is, at least, unbecoming.

You might save the situation by first saying, "please excuse me, but I must quickly catch this person, and I promise to be right back with you." If you do not do that, even though you may think the lack of protocol is minor, it may hurt feelings. It might also be observed by others and could appear to be a bit insensitive to anyone who may notice. Treat each person as if they were important because they are.

Have you ever approached a retail store only to hear a voice out of nowhere, say, "Welcome to our store?" Not only is no one making eye contact with you, but you would need a road map and a compass to find their location! The voice may just as well be saying "Hello, Earthling! Welcome to our planet."

Although this was meant to be a friendly greeting, a greeting coming as though from a starship orbiting one of Jupiter's moons does not a happy and friendly greeting make if you are the human on earth wondering from whence the voice you are faintly hearing is coming.

Here is an example of what does work. When I attend weekly worship services in my neighborhood, there is a friendly greeter standing inside the door. Even though now 90 years old, he looks you in the eye, says hello, welcomes you with a smile as big as eternity and then gives you a great big hug. Then, and only then, does he give you a program for that week's service. He always says, "It's good to see you."

I went home for Christmas this year to visit my family. On Sunday, my brother drove me to the local place of worship several miles away. I looked for a greeter standing by the door. There was none. I found myself looking several times. I wanted to see my 90 year-old friend. I wanted a hug. I wanted a greeter.

Shake Hands

When you shake someone's hand, shake it with a firm grip to let them know you are alive. When you shake hands with some folks, it feels as though their hand is a wet noodle or a freshly caught Rainbow Trout. Don' be a wet noodle or a Rainbow Trout.

Smile

Smile, and people will get the idea that you are friendly, likeable and approachable. If you frown, the natural instinct of others will be to turn away. A smile invites people in, while a frown can scare them away.

I asked one older gentleman, "are you happy?" He said: "Oh I'm happy enough, I just don't see too good anymore... need these bifocals to see up close. I have this new hearing aid, but I still can barely hear. The hair that was once on the top of my head first turned grey, then it all fell out." I asked, "Don't have any more lawn up there to mow or fertilize, eh? But are you happy sir?" "Sure, I'm happy enough."

I didn't say this to him but I thought, "Then why don't you try telling the frown on your face that you are happy, because your constant and ever-present frown is starting to alienate people. Why don't we just order you a brand new head? Then you can have new eyes, new ears, thick curly hair, like Sampson, and we'll order you one that comes with a permanent smile!" If someone has a beautiful smile, say so, but you must be genuine and sincere. If you are not, even children, it seems, can tell.

Say Hello

After you begin your greeting with eye contact and a smile, then say hello. Some people just haven't learned how to comfortably greet others. They might have a small group with whom they relate and feel comfortable, but saying hello to strangers is just uncomfortable.

I was shocked when I walked past someone while shopping a while back. He stopped me and said, "I haven't seen you for a while." I had seen this person several times a week for seven years in the same place, and he never bothered to even acknowledge me.

I said: "I have changed my schedule," then I sat down on his bench and we visited for a moment. When one of his family members arrived he did not utter these words, but I could feel the sentiment: "I have to go. You have had all the attention I can give you for now, talk to you in another seven years!"

Introduce Yourself

When you meet someone for the first

time, tell them your name. Think about your favorite book or movie. Now imagine for a moment what it would be like if the super hero or main character was never ultimately given a name. It would just not be the same.

In fact, Super Man was actually given two names: *Clark Kent, mild mannered reporter, and Super Man, man of steel.* You have a name of course, and it should be just as prominently presented to others as if you were famous. Tell your name to those you meet.

Ask the Name of Your New Acquaintance

Also, when you meet someone new, ask their name, and try to immediately memorize it by repeating it once or twice to them. When you re-visit those you have previously met, use their name each time you see them.

People appreciate hearing their names spoken. It is more important to them than you may imagine! If you are not sure how to pronounce it, ask them how it is pronounced when you first meet them, then say it back to them to make sure you get it right. Then try to remember it.

Say the name over and over again in your mind when speaking with them if you are just learning the name. Write it down when you are alone, and take some notes to help you remember. The person will be impressed that you remember their name when you see them again. Also, a very nice thing to say, and have people hear, when you first meet, is: "I hope to see you again."

This will make the other individual feel as though you care about them. They will certainly get the idea that you have more than just noticed them.

For Youth

When you say hello to those you don't know, ask their names, say their names, then repeat their names each time you see them. When you do this, those you are just getting to know will often become your friends. Saying "hi Jim," "hi Greg," "hello Mary," or "hello Betty," may even help your relationship blossom into something special, and you might acquire your first boy or girl friend.

Saying, "hello Jim," when the person's name is actually Henry, may not work, unless in obvious jest, but exhibiting a sense of humor often will. One of my friends who was loved by all, before his passing, used to say to obvious non smokers, he was seating in a non-smoking building, "this is the non-smoking section." Everyone loved him the more for it, knowing he intended it for their pleasure.

What to Do When Meeting Someone New

If you are a young lady, and a new girl should move in nearby, you may want to walk over and introduce yourself. You could say, "Hi I'm Betty, or whatever your name may be, and I just live across the street. My friends and I are going to the park to play, and we thought you might like to come with us. I have a new electric skateboard. You can take a turn on it if you want."

Should a new girl suddenly appear at your high school and you learn she has moved there from a foreign country, she would probably be worried about being accepted and making new friends. If you were to invite her to sit with you in the cafeteria for lunch, then tell her all about the next school dance, she would surely be grateful. Then if you were to tell the "guys" about her and ask if one of them would be willing to invite her to the dance, that would be going the extra mile, and you would likely make a new friend.

What to Say When Meeting Someone New

One of my friends told me recently that the way he has become acquainted with people from all over the world is by simply asking,

"Where are you from?" A young man stopped me in a parking lot a while ago and said, " I love your collector car." That allowed me to meet his wife, his mother and his entire family who were with him, and we have since become good friends.

When a friend saw a young girl about seven years old struggling with the ice cream machine in a restaurant a few nights ago, he simply asked, "May I help you?" When she answered yes, he discovered that the strawberry dispenser was broken.

He helped her to get some chocolate and vanilla ice cream instead, then gave here a real strawberry on a stick, and showed her how to cover it with chocolate from the circling chocolate machine. This friendly act, also allowed him to meet her family. Asking, "May I help you?" can work with people of all ages.

Sharing Talents

By offering to share your talents, you will be able to meet even more people and make more friends. For example, by saying, "Excuse me, Betty. My name is Sherrie. I'm in your homemaking class. I sure wish I could bake chocolate chip cookies the way you do. I'm pretty good with hair and make-up. If you'll show me how to make chocolate chip cookies, I'll show you how to wear your hair and make-up just like Princess Leah."

You could also say, "Excuse me, Jim, isn't it? I'm Bob. I watch all of your basketball games, and I really wish I could shoot the way you do. I'm in your chemistry class. I'm having good success there, and you have implied you struggle a little with it. If you will show me how to better shoot baskets, I'll be happy to help you with your chemistry."

There are no special formulas when it comes to meeting and interacting with others. However, if you make the other person feel important and respected, there will often be a good result. Just do what works for you and be yourself.

The Power of Please and Thank You

Recently, I came across some scriptures on being thankful:

"Praise the Lord! Oh give thanks to the Lord, for he is good, for his steadfast love endures forever! Who can utter the mighty deeds of the Lord, or declare all his praise" (Psalm 106:1-2)?

"Give thanks in all circumstances; for this is the will of God in Christ Jesus for you" (2 Thessalonians 5:18).

Then I remembered the words to a favorite hymn, "Count Your Many Blessings." I decided to try something new with my personal prayers. Instead of praying for what I needed, I decided to say, "thank you" for what I already had, for an entire week.

It was not easy to do at first because the natural human tendency is to think of oneself and to ask for those things that we need. However, I began by saying, "thank you for the air I breathe. Thank you for allowing me to be alive and to live in this beautiful world you have made."

That's about as far as I would get, then my mind would shift to the things I needed and I would ask for blessings relating to family, friends and neighbors. By the end of the week, I found I could get through my entire prayers saying only, "thank you," for so many things.

Having finished a week of praying that way, I decided to begin another week differently. I began by saying, "thank you," and then I would only ask to be able to help others and not even mention what I needed. That exercise filled my heart with gratitude, and allowed me to feel a sense of peace and confidence greater than I had felt before.

There is nothing wrong with praying for the things we need and we should certainly do that, but when we put the emphasis on being thankful and helping and caring for others, everything changes. From the scriptures we have the following:

"First of all, then, I urge that supplications, prayers, intercessions, and thanksgivings be made for all people" (1Timothy 2: 1).

"Rejoice in the Lord always, again I will say, Rejoice. Let your reasonableness be known to everyone.

The Lord is at hand; do not be anxious about anything, but in everything by prayer and supplication with thanksgiving let your requests be made know to God. And the peace of God, which surpasses all understanding, will guard your hearts and your minds in Christ Jesus" (Philippians 4:4-7).

How to Say Please

The word "please" softens the act of asking someone to perform a beneficial act on your behalf, and there is more than one way to say it. You can say, "I wonder if you could please do this" or, "when you get a minute, could you do this?" You could also say, "Would you be so kind as to do this or that?" Communicating in this way allows the person you are asking to feel as though it is their decision to help you, and this politeness also tends to soften the heart of those receiving the request.

Learn to Say Please and Thank You in Many Languages

If you take the time to learn how to say please and thank you in multiple languages, you will find that saying those three little words could pay big dividends. Showing this real appreciation and respect for the others, will open more doors for you than your own personal doorman. You may even find yourself in the company of various important individuals when such could be especially helpful.

To learn to say these simple but powerful words in many languages, go to Maholo.com and youtube.com. There, you will learn to pronounce those words in many languages perfectly.

To say please in Spanish one may say, "por favor." I like the Spanish expression, "con permission," which translates as, "If you will excuse me," or simply, "excuse me." To say, thank you in Spanish, say "gracias,' for thanks, or "muchas gracias" for "thank you very much. When the French say please, they say: "s'il- vous-plais," which translates: "if it pleases you." I like that because it shows respect and consideration for others. When the French say thank you, they say: "merci" for thanks, or "merci beaucoup" for thank you very much.

When Italians say please, they say: "per favore" which is pronounced, "pair-fah-voh-ray." When Italians wish to thank someone they say: "grazie" which is pronounced, "grat-see-eh."

When you use that word in Italian, you are wishing people graces. For Italians, gratitude can never be excessive, the more the merrier. So when you wish to express extreme gratitude to someone in Italian say: "grazie mille" which translates as, "a thousand graces.

When German-speaking people say thank you, they say: "Danke." To say thank you very much, say: "Danke Schon." If you wish to say please in German, you would say:" bitte." It is pronounced "bitteh." This word is also used to say you're welcome.

To say please in Russian just say: "poh-shzah-loo-stah." To say thank you in Russian, say: "spah.see-boh." To say please in Mandarin Chinese say: "Qing." When Mandarin Chinese people say thank you, they say: xie xie. One would pronounce xie xie as "syeh-syeh." The first xie begins high and then drops at the end. The second xie is said lightly and without emphasis. "Domo arigato gozaimasu"…is the more formal form in Japanese for, "thank you very much." To say please in Japanese, say: "kudasai."

You're Welcome

When someone says, "thank you," it would be appropriate and desirable for you to respond by saying, "you're welcome."

To say you're welcome in French say, "de rien" or "avec pleasure." To say you're welcome in Italian say, "prego." When speaking German say, "bitte" or to say you're welcome very much you may say, "bitte shon." If you wish to say you're welcome in Spanish you would say, "de nada." If you are speaking Russian you would say, "pazhaloosta."

The Chinese say you're welcome by saying, "shou huanyding de." If you wish to say you're welcome in Japanese you may say, "do itashimashite" for the formal way. For the less formal way just say, "donmai" which is a transliteration into Japanese of "don't mind it."

The Use of Language

I was in a grocery store some years ago looking for yogurt. I asked a gentleman walking past me, "where is the yogurt at, please." The nice man I had asked looked at me with great disappointment and said, "ouch, my ears!" He then said, "You don't want to say that. Instead, try saying, excuse me sir, can you tell me where the yogurt is located." That nice gentleman turned out to be a college English professor and I thanked him for correcting me.

At the same time, I thought to myself, "Did you say that? You know how to speak better than that." But when we get in a hurry, and speak without stopping to think what we are about to say, it is easy to use slang or to speak incorrectly. I can't help but wonder what we all might hear if we would record our conversations for just one day!

You're Fine and I'm Good

A visitor from one of the eastern states said to me: "You folks sure do talk funny out your way. You say crick instead of creek. My favorite is that you are constantly saying, "you're fine and I'm good."

Our preacher just preached a sermon about not saying, 'I'm good' and here you folks are saying it all the time." It turns out, the person visiting from back east was correct. We do say, "I'm good, "often. How do I know? I found myself saying, the words just the other day. When the words left my mouth, I thought, "Stop first and think before you speak."

Doing Good Vs. Being Good ("Colloquialisms")

Colloquialisms can represent an aberration in correct speech that is sometimes done deliberately for effect, but also is often adopted innocently by the general populace without even recognizing that they're speaking incorrect English. This, in turn, can put others off, if the listener realizes the difference, and they in turn, can often impute a lack of knowledge or refinement to the speaker.

Having fun with words, as with puns, and other deliberate twists of words, thus conveying humor, can often be endearing, and can even occasionally show you are one of the "in group," so to speak. Thus, there can be some redeeming features to this practice, but don't be caught in the position, especially with a prospective employer, for example, of using colloquialisms or other incorrect English unknowingly. It may well lose you a desired professional position.

In an entirely different context, and more as an observation than a direction, if we want to be very selective about word usage in a religious setting, for example, we could even quibble about words or phrases that we all use ever day, that could be classically and historically somewhat inappropriate, if we are being very meticulous.

For example, again in this very specific context, there is a difference between being good, and doing good deeds. In the New Testament, a man came running, kneeling before Jesus and asked him a question after addressing him as "Good Master."

Jesus answering him said: "Why callest thou me good? There is none good but one, that is, God" (Mark 10:18). In this very limited context, we could take care and realize that saying "I'm good," or "you're good," or calling people "good" or answering "good" when someone asks us how we are doing might even there, reflect an impropriety, if being very sensitive in the particular context.

However, Jesus also taught us: "Be ye therefore perfect, even as your Father which is in heaven is perfect" (Matthew 5:48). Jesus would have us seek perfection and do good things but always retain in remembrance that we are not perfect yet.

Therefore, we should remain humble but seek to do good works knowing there is only one that is perfect and thereby good, and that is God.

Doing good deeds can typically be a preferred way to live in many societies. Some may even be surprised to discover that such behavior can be very personally rewarding, or in a more youthful vernacular, "fun." But, in a specifically religious context, some would remind to not forget from where all good comes.

Herein, it could be maintained that all good things come from God. "Every good gift and every perfect gift is from above, and cometh down from the Father of lights, with whom there is no variableness, neither shadow of turning" (James 1:17).

The idea and process of doing kind acts, for example, to help, nourish, love and care for all of God's children, comes from God and not man. God has put those feelings in the hearts of men. So don't let your neighbors have all the fun in doing the kind acts of helping, loving, and caring for others. There are plenty of kind acts and good deeds left to do, for all.

Here is one of my favorite ways to answer the person who asks you, "How are you doing today?" Without ever using the words, "I'm good, good, or everybody is good." Just say: "I am scintillating, fascinating and sometimes effervescing. But I don't effervesce all of the time; just when I have an epiphany, then watch out!"

One Hundred and Forty-Four Ways
to Tell People How You Are Doing

You may wish to also have fun using any one of the following one hundred and forty-four more replies: "If life gives you lemons, make lemonade; *No worries mate*; **I am well thank you.** I am blessed; I am *Peachy keen; Hunky dory*. **Life is a bowl of cherries.** Marvelous, Awesome, Fantastic, Excellent, Too right. **Not too badly actually,** Not too bad; **Sensational,** Swell, I'm on my way to heaven. Delightful, Better than ever; Knockin' em dead; Fair to medlin', Mystifyin; Captivating. **Fabulous**. So nice, Ain't life grand? Pure gold, Golden, Singin' and humin, Playin' with the big boys. It's a wonderful life.

Fortunate. Outstanding, **Terrific.**

Soaring with the eagles, Filled with merriment, **Exceptional.** *You ain't seen nothin' yet, Life is a hoot, Life is a beautiful thing. About right, Life is nice. All is well. Super. Sometimes I'm up sometimes I'm down but I'll-always be around. I will survive. Feelin' so nice,* **Feeling blessed**, *I get a kick out of life. Content as a rainbow after a spring rain. Grateful to be alive, Feelin' all right, Cheerful, Positively resplendent.*

Sparklin' like the stars at night. *Life is a dream. Life is delicious, Happy. Life is fascinating, Better than I deserve, Groovin' with the feelin,' Shakin' and a bakin,' I've got my mojo workin,' Bein' all I can be, Practically in heaven. Rockin' and a rollin,' Passionate about perfection. Feelin' glad all over.*

Gleeful, *I am feelin' so right. Just heavenly, It's fun to be alive, Amazing-life is amazing. Uptight outta sight and all right.* **Picture perfect**, *I am so far out-I'm gone. Life is practically perfect. Bodacious. Wonderful. Remarkable.* **Exuberant.**

I'm punctuated with poetry, harmony and song. Fearless today, Parsimonious but only sometimes. Resolute, Stupendous, Whimsical, **Victorious,** *Vivacious from time to time, Lookin' for even better days. Feeling like cherry blossoms in springtime. If life get's any better I just might explode. I was lugubrious but I got over it.*

Life is a Miracle! *Goin' with the flow daddy-o, Oakley dokali. I've got it goin' on, I've just got to say in every way-I dig life! Life is sweet, Groovy,* **Sensational,** *Life is a sweet sensation- Can I get a witness? Incredible, Better than yesterday, Ask me on the weekend.*

I'm cookin' with gas. Life is mostly sunny days. Life is a touchdown-a homerun and a slam-dunk all rolled into one. Fit as a fiddle, I repeat- life is sweet. **I'm all the better for seeing you.**

I'm happy and excited just to be alive. Dreamin' of those sunny skies. Hopeful. Carefree. Improving one day at a time. **Optimistic.** *Changing for the better-one day at a time. I'm well done son. Better than yesterday,* **Feeling blissful today.**

Couldn't be better, Feelin' fortuitous. Life is one sunny day, Totally cool. I feel like a kid in a candy store. It's comin' up rainbows, Life is beautilicious. I've got my zing back, **Stupendous***, Feelin' glad all over. Right as rain. Ain't no denyin'- life is- electrifyin'. Think I've found heaven on earth. Life is, la ti da, Hot diggity dog! It's comin' up roses.*

Life is a holiduy, Life is, a celebration. Feeling merry. I'm living in a state of constant and total amazement. **Life is a wonder- ment!"**

You're Fine

There is another catch phrase that has invaded Utah and other parts of America like the bubonic plague once invaded Europe. Besides saying, "I'm good," we also say, "You're fine!" (supposedly meaning there is nothing about which you need to be concerned). What does that even mean, "You're fine?"

I know what, "She's so fine, my 409," means. The Beach Boys sang about the new Chevy Impala of the early 1960's that had an engine packed with four hundred and nine cubic inches of raw power back then. But do the people who use the phrase, "You're fine," even know what they are trying to say themselves?

I finally figured out what I think they are trying to say. They are trying to say, "It's all right sir or madam. It is no big deal." Years ago, one used to hear, "no biggie!" or, "don't sweat the small stuff." But people today are not saying that.

I can remember not too long ago people were saying, "no prob.," Or even "no problemo," which was another way of saying: "no problem." Some used to say, "no big whop." But what is this "you're fine, business?" It's not working Myrtle. I can understand your turtle better than I can understand you.

If we keep on saying, "I'm fine, you're fine, and I'm good, she's good, everybody's good," we will be sounding just like the Pharisee who went up into the temple to pray. For the sake of illustration, in today's language, Mr. Pharisee may have spoken like this: "Now when it comes to being good, I tell you what, I am good! Yippee ki yay and whoop-te-doo, I am good!

Why I'm so good, I can hardly believe it myself. I fast twice a week, I pay my tithes and by the way, I am so glad I am not like this miserable sinning publican. Thank you, and Amen."

And now for a reality check: We all could be more like the publican who said, "God be merciful to me, a sinner" (Luke 18:13).

It's Like

Two young ladies were walking behind me this morning and one of them said, "it's like what?" Then the other one said, "she was like," and, "I was like." Then one of them said, "it's like, you know what I mean?"

Let me just say: "hold the phone Mabel. No one knows what you mean because you have yet to say anything." So next time you are about to begin speaking and misuse the word, "like" please stop, count to ten, take a minute to consider what you might say without ever using the word, "like." You may even wish to use the word like to create a simile, which is one of the reasons, the word, "like" exists.

A simile is a direct comparison between two different things using the words like and as. For example: "Life is like the rain, sometimes it gets you all wet and sometimes it brings rainbows."

Jesus used simile when he spoke about the scribes and the Pharisees being hypocrites. The Savior said: "Ye are like unto whited sepulchres, which outwardly appear beautiful but inside are full of dead men's bones and all uncleanliness" (Matthew 23:27).

Saying "it's like," "she was like," "he was like" and "you know what I mean" will not keep you out of heaven.

You will not be swearing or taking the Lord's name in vain. Neither will you be breaking any of man's laws. Speaking thus, is after all, the "in thing" to do. It may help you to be more popular and fit in with the crowd.

However, for those who do the hiring and for others who are looking for future leaders, you will be immediately discovered as soon as they here you speak. Some who listen to you speak may even consider you uneducated and simple minded. You have a choice to let the world know you can speak properly. It may be wise to do so.

Choose Your Words Carefully

I was recently at a gathering of people when the man conducting asked if any one else would be coming to the meeting. One lady said, "There was another guy here but he just left." It would have sounded so much more respectful and dignified and would have shown so much more consideration for all in attendance if the lady speaking had said: "there was another "gentleman" here but he just left." Words are just little things but they carry great power!

Especially for Children

When you finish playing with your bicycle, tricycle or skateboard, please store them in your garage. Do not leave them in the path leading to your front door or on the front porch steps in front of your door. Someone may not see them and trip and fall. Should you have to leave these items in the front yard, be sure you secure them to something that is solid and immovable with a chain and lock to insure they will not be stolen.

Years ago, two children from my neighborhood I had grown to love were given instructions by me, on the importance of keeping their bicycles locked when they were not being used. One was given a new lock and chain and the other was found to already have one.

One day, following a late lunch with a friend we both discovered their bicycles lying on the neighbor's lawn across the street from my home. I decided to have my friend help me hide their bicycles in my garage for a couple of days and nights.

When the children came to me and told me their bikes were missing, I asked them if they had used their locks and chains to secure their bicycles to some immovable object. They both looked at me with the same look a puppy has when he knows he has done something wrong. After two days, I returned the children's bicycles and reminded them once again, to lock their bikes with their locks and chains to anything that would not move.

Be Considerate

When you and your friends visit the park to play football, soccer and baseball, do not park your bicycles on the surrounding sidewalks that others use. Be considerate of others who may wish to use the sidewalks to move about the park or other places having sidewalks, including in front of your own home.

Should you get in the habit of being inconsiderate in this way, you may grow up to be an adult who will park in handicapped parking that is reserved for the truly handicapped, such as American veterans who have lost limbs to defend our country. I did that once in Phoenix, just long enough to stop and pick up a pizza but it was long enough for someone to notice and call me on it. I do not intend to do that ever again.

Be Nice

My friend, who is also my mechanic, invited me to visit him about 40 miles away. He wanted to show me the dirt bike he had on "lay away" to give to his older boy for Christmas. When I arrived, he had just called the boy who would receive the gift, (about 10 or 11 years old) into the living room.

When I sat down, the father began talking to him about cleaning his room. I asked the father's permission to talk to the boy for a minute and to ask him one question. I began by saying, "you know Santa Claus will be coming soon and he keeps a list of who has been naughty and who has been nice. I have one question for you, "HAVE YOU BEEN NICE?"

The look on the boy's face changed. He became very serious. He was on the spot. He said, "Well, I guess so." I asked the question again. "Have you truly been nice?" He said, "I guess I could be nicer."

His father then called the younger boy, about seven years old into the living room. The older boy immediately said, "Don't try lying to this guy; you won't get away with it."

Keep Your Room Clean

I took the youngest boy into his room and following a little direction, and after two tries, he made a fine job of cleaning his room. (There are so many children in this world who do not have their own bedroom. Please keep yours clean and orderly at all times).

The father and I then went to the store where the older boy's dirt bike was waiting. It was a great bike. The younger boy had his Christmas presents also hiding in another place waiting for him. So if you want to have a great Christmas, be nice. And don't try telling little white lies when a grown-up asks you if you have truly been nice.

Never Tell Any Lies

The mother of one of my friends called to tell me a story about her stepdaughter. The school principal had just called, to explain that her stepdaughter had invented a lie about her leg hurting her so terribly, that she would need to go home early that day and maybe stay home for a week or more.

The stepmother told the principal to let her come home, that she would be there directly to pick her up, and that she would take care of the situation. I was invited to accompany the stepmother to retrieve the girl, who was then, ten years old.

On the way back home, an idea came to me like a bolt of lightening. I asked the stepmother to stop at the entrance of the emergency hospital on our way home. I asked her to keep the girl in the car with her and wait until I returned. I knew at least one doctor who worked in the emergency room and hoped he would be working that day.

When I walked back inside, with the girl and her stepmother, the doctor was waiting to meet us and he escorted the young girl into the emergency room. The doctor examined the supposed ailing leg, complete with the knee reflex test. The doctor looked at the girl intently and then said, "I have bad news for you, your leg will have to come off."

The girl was caught completely off guard. She did not know what to think, but she knew she had been caught telling a lie. Or, was there something really wrong with her leg after all?

The doctor said, "I'll be right back." In just a few moments, the doctor returned wearing his operating clothing complete with an operating mask and a light at the top of his head and carrying a operating saw in his right hand. The scene looked like something out of a movie. The doctor said, "I'll have to operate immediately."

The girl took one look at that scene and turned white with terror. When the doctor moved the operating saw toward her leg, she began screaming loud enough to be heard a block away. Her stepmother calmed her down and then said, "Don't you ever lie to me again, young lady." And we hope she never did.

Share Your Toys and Help Your Friends

When you share your toys, you will be learning to be young ladies and gentlemen. Should you never share your toys or help your friends, you may never become ladies and gentlemen.

When I was in grade school, I was having trouble with division. I asked one of my friends to help me. He came over after school for several days and patiently taught me how to do division. I invited him to play cowboys and Indians with us in our back yard. He didn't know how to make a bow with arrows, so I taught him how to do that and everyone was happy.

Copy the Love Your Mother Has for You

When I was, perhaps, six or seven years of age, I decided I would run away from home. I managed to get five houses away and sought refuge in our schoolyard. I sat down on the cement sidewalk in front of one of the grade school classes, and leaned my back against the brick wall. The fenced playground was in front of me, covered with sand.

I can remember thinking, "I'll show them who is boss. I'll show them I can take care of myself." It wasn't long until a station wagon pulled up next to the classroom and a lady I recognized got out of the car and walked up to me. It was one of our neighbors and a friend of my mother. She said, "Your mother is worried sick about you. You should never run away from home. We'd better get you back home right away."

Now, years later, I am the one who is sick but it is a different kind of sick. I am not "worried sick," but when I think of doing that to my angel mother, I get a sickening feeling in my stomach and my heart aches. Emulate the love your mother has for you. Copy that kind of love with others. Model yourself after your mother's love for you. There is no greater love on this earth than a mother's love for her children.

Don't Forget to Pray

When you are frightened and have lost your way, don't forget to pray. A little girl shared in one of our worship services that one day when she arrived home from school, her house key was missing. She was alone and no one was home. She got down on her knees and prayed for God to help her. She looked everywhere for the lost house key. She found it hiding in the front yard lawn and was able to enter the safety of her home.

Never think, even for one moment, that God does not love you. God loves you and God cares about you. God made you. We are all God's children, even your mommy and daddy. God knows your name and God knows everything about you. God wants you to pray to him and ask for his help whenever you need help and whenever you have a question about anything. Don' forget to say your morning prayers and evening prayers.

When I was a boy, this prayer was popular:

"Now I lay me down to sleep.
I pray the Lord my soul to keep;
If I die before I wake,
I pray the Lord, my soul to take. Amen"

Children know, in who's holy name they finish their prayers and they know how to say, Amen. They even know they pray to their Heavenly Father.

From all of the times I have been able to hear children pray in public, I have yet to hear children not thank their Heavenly Father for those things which they have. Unless it is something that has frightened them as in the example of the "lost house-key" above, children also seem to always be praying for others and not themselves.

We adults could learn a great deal from listening to the innocent, beautiful and powerful prayers of children.

Jesus taught, "But when ye pray, use not vain repetitions," (Matthew 6:7). That means not to say the same thing each time you pray. God gave you your own mind, heart, and thoughts. Speak that which is in your heart and use your own words when you pray. God will always answer the humble prayer of a child's heart. That is why he would like us grown-ups to become more humble and child-like.

I can remember my sister Patty praying as a child. I could hear her prayers through the bedroom wall which was connected to mine, and that would always remind me to say my prayers.

I do not remember how old she was when her praying each night began. My best guess is that she was four years old. I was eleven years older. I do not remember the words of her prayers. I am sure she followed the pattern of children praying just mentioned, because she has always had a kind and loving heart. I do remember how proud I was of my little sister for praying out loud each evening, using her own words, before she went to sleep.

Communicating with Others Respectfully

By the time I was a high school senior, I had barely turned 16 years of age. This age presented no problems at all for me as a mighty senior because I had attended the same high school with those a year or more ahead of me since the eighth grade.

I had plenty of time to get to know and make friends with many of the guys who were a year or two ahead of me.

But as a 15 year-old high school junior, my age difference could have presented a big problem, because the high school seniors I had to live with every day were 18, 18 and a half and several were already 19 years old. There is a huge difference between the physical maturity of a fifteen year-old, and a19 year-old. Just ask anyone in that situation.

Some high school seniors have the definite tendency to flaunt the fact that they are mighty seniors. Treating the younger students around them with a daily dose of disrespect can be a way of life for them. Everyone knows that bullies exist. They come in all colors, and sizes and they can be young or older boys or girls. I like Webster's 1913 definition of a bully: "A noisy, blustering fellow, more insolent than courageous, who threatens, intimidates, or badgers people who are smaller or weaker than he is, an insolent, tyrannical fellow."

It will never serve us well to treat any of God's children disrespectfully. If animals can show us that they have had their feelings hurt, then certainly children of all ages and older young ladies and gentlemen can have their feelings hurt. We should all be careful not only with what we do, but with what we say to those around us. It is entirely possible for a young person to say something without thinking first, that will hurt another young person's feelings so profoundly that those memories will last well into adulthood.

      Young men and women can also pull pranks on one another which seem innocent and harmless enough at the time, but sometimes such thoughtless and even stupid acts will embarrass and humiliate those on the receiving end, to the extent that the memories of such will last well into adulthood. Always think first, of the other person before you do or say anything that may hurt them. We are not in the business of tearing people down, but of lifting all of God's children up!

      Do not speak to someone as if they were six years old unless they are six years old. If you do that, you will appear to be six years old in the eyes of the other person. Whether you know it or not, the person you will be talking to will know how to do something you do not know how to do. He will have at least one talent and one gift of the spirit given to him by God. And whether you remember it or not that person will also be a child of God!

When you speak with someone on the phone, state your name and the name of your business if it is a business call; otherwise just saying your name will do, and then pause and ask the person how they are doing or how their day is going. While making business calls, I have had people say many times, "thank you for asking. You are the only person who has asked me that this week."

Why We Should Not Condemn

We should never condemn others. Our job is to lift others up and to help and assist them in becoming better. One should also know when to speak and when to hold one's peace. A friend once told me about an experience at a meeting. People at the meeting were praising a certain person for the good things he had done. Those in the meeting were considering doing business with this individual. My friend said: "I knew this person had taken advantage of certain others."

He said he thought about speaking up, but did not say anything. In the next moment, the person conducting the meeting said to him, "you know you are a lot like this person." My friend, told me he would have never heard those kind words spoken about himself, had he said anything about the other person.

Know When to Stop Talking and Listen

Know when to stop talking. When the person you are speaking to stops listening, it is time to stop talking. If they look away while you are speaking to them, they have probably lost interest in what you have to say, and it will be time for you to stop talking. When you are speaking with another person, it is sometimes a great idea to just stop talking altogether and listen to them.

Very recently, I had the extreme pleasure of meeting a medical professional for the first time. The moment this person began speaking, I detected a southern accent. I guessed which state she was from and that pleased both of us. I decided to just be still and let this person speak. When we parted company, I noticed that she had been doing almost all of the talking for more than 40 minutes. She even said to me, "I haven't told that to anyone except my own family." When our visit ended, I knew more about this new friend than I do about some of my neighbors who have lived around me for more than 20 years!

Continuing now with the idea of letting the other lady or fellow, do the talking, I recently, found myself on an airplane sitting next to a gentleman with an empty seat between us. Had I followed my usual approach, I would not only have been the first one to speak, but would have been the one to say something to try and make his life better.

This time, I had the impression to just be still and wait on him. He began by introducing himself. He then offered me some earplugs. When the flight was about to end, he asked me if he could offer a prayer in my behalf! Then he left me with his phone number and said if I ever found myself where he lived, to look him up.

Any time someone offers to pray for you, let them pray for you. Jesus said: "for he that is not against us is for us" (Luke 9:50). That is so true. All of that happened because I let the other "fella" do the talking.

Let People Know You Care About Them

Let the other person know you care about them. I have been doing business over the phone for more than 20 years. Most of the customers who call to make orders have never met me in person, and I have yet to see most of them up close. I have always tried to let the customer know I care about them by asking the simplest questions. For example, "how is life treating you these days?"

Not long ago, a customer called and said, "I hope you will forgive me for not ordering at this time." I could tell immediately that he just needed to talk, so I said, "of course, it's good to hear from you." He had called to tell me that his brother had recently died, and he did, indeed, need to talk.

Thankfully, there was only one call that interrupted us, and I asked that person if I could call them back. I can't tell you if this man talked for twenty minutes or for forty minutes, I wasn't counting the time. This gentleman needed to talk, and I needed to listen, and we were both blessed.

If you don't have something good to say about someone, do not say anything. I mentioned that to one person when he began talking about someone quite critically. He said, "I guess you won't be hearing another word out of me for a while!"

"Good Luck"

Concerning our communicating with one another: Sometimes we may say things or use expressions that we do not necessarily mean. For example, when the expression, "good luck," is used, it is generally well intended and well received. The intended meaning is: "(I or we) wish you great success with your next endeavor." Perhaps a different choice of words would be even more effective.

However, Since luck in the true sense is often associated with Las Vegas and Vegas is associated with gamboling, those who love the Lord may wish to distance themselves from using the phrase: "good luck, " which is used as a part of every day speech in our language. The French have it right when they say: "Bon chance" which interpreted, means: good chance, which interpreted even further really means: "we wish you well with the law of averages."

Strictly speaking, there is no such thing as luck, but only, the law of averages. The words, "good luck" have simply become an expression of our language. When well-meaning people use the expression, "good luck" we hope they mean: "we wish you a good outcome in your next and latest endeavor."

Unfortunately, the expression is also deeply steeped in a different meaning. Good luck also implies, "we hope you win at a roll of the dice or a turn of the cards or a pull at the slot machines or a bet on your next sports team or business deal." "We hope you win lots of money with no effort from you, except laying your money down."

In a way, the expression, "good luck" is a near perfect example of how the devil takes what may have started out as a perfectly innocent expression, and taints and changes it to imply and mean something completely different.

When these words leave the mouth of one who loves God, it seems to me the same as going to a fountain and expecting to get clean pure, and refreshing water, and having the fountain spout forth gasoline or some other toxic material instead. For those of us who love the Lord, let us consider removing the phrase "good luck" from our language and replacing it with, "we wish you well with your next endeavor," or, "may God go with you," or you may wish to say, "God bless you until we meet again," or simply, "blessings to you."

If a phrase does not inspire us to do good and believe in Christ, and saying "good luck" does not, then we might as well use any other phrase that promotes anti-social behavior, or even evil. If "good luck" is interpreted as promoting games of chance, is that really what we would wish on others? In their worst form, these activities; could be seen by some as promoting evil.

Far be it from us to wish such on anyone. Evil doing especially pleases one person in particular. He is Satan or the Devil, who is the father of all lies, and saying, "good luck" could fit right in with his desires.

Not one lie and nothing that causes confusion originated with man. Satan was lying and confusing our father Adam and his sons and daughters long before you were born. The devil is the father of all lies and the author of all confusion. (See John 8:44 and 1 Corinthians 14:33).

Integrity and Honor

If you give your word to someone to do something, keep your word and your honor and do what you said you would do. Today, when someone says they will do something, one can never be certain whether they will do the thing or not.

Back in Old Testament times, people reinforced their word or their promise to do something by taking an oath. It is not so today. Should you not be sure you can do something, it would be better to decline at the onset than to leave the other fella hanging hoping you will do the thing. Remember you have the right to say no.

One of my friends is a retired two-star Air Force general. He recently told me this story: While backing out of his parking space, he managed to back his pick-up truck into another car. He immediately got out of his vehicle and walked up to the driver of the damaged car and said: "Please excuse me, let me give you my name and phone number and the name and number of my insurance company and we will make this right for you."

What should you do if you put a dent or a ding in another parked car and there is no one around to see you do it? Do you drive away hoping not to get caught? You had better not try that. There are cameras everywhere these days.

There are surveillance cameras out there and every smart phone seems to have a built in camera.

You should leave a note on the person's windshield with your name and phone number and tell them you are the one who hit their car and you will be the one to make it right. Besides, if a human doesn't see you, God will. Remember, we are here to be tested and angels are silently note taking. Let's try our best to be sure the report they make of us is a good one.

Treating People the Way God Would Have Us Treat Them

I often hear people say: "Oh, I love the man all right, I just don't like him. Can't stand him if the truth be told." But to tell you the truth in the spirit of friendly instruction, you had better get to like him because liking someone should always precede loving them. How can you possibly love someone if you don't even like them?

If that ever happens to you, that will be the time to do some serious praying until you can begin to see the good in that person and ask God to help you learn to like the person you can't stand. Have you ever considered that the person you can't stand may find something about you that he can't stand either?

In any case, the test for all of us who claim to be followers of Jesus Christ is to love one another. Jesus said: "By this shall all men know that ye are my disciples, if ye have love one to another" (John 13:35).

Give Hugs

Give hugs! Now for a little homespun wisdom: Giving hugs will increase the lifespan of both the giver and the receiver. Not long ago, a little girl I have known since her birth invited me to be present during her upcoming rite of passage. She had reached the required age, and family and friends were invited to celebrate with her. I arrived early to get a front row seat. As people began to arrive, she walked up to each one and gave them a big hug and thanked them for coming.

Her mommy and daddy did not tell her to do this, she figured it out all on her own. Just a short time ago someone sneaked up behind me and gave me a big hug. It turned out to be someone I had not seen in more than 20 years! Just last week someone hugged me and then looked deep into my eyes and said, "it's always better when you are here." When was the last time you gave somebody a hug? Giving hugs will increase the lifespan of both the giver and the receiver. I really believe that.

How to Ask for Help

When you need someone's help, always ask for it when it is convenient *for them*. Then, never forget to thank them in advance, and then again, *after* they have done something for you. Gratitude is a highly underrated necessity of life!

The way you treat people, will determine how you will be treated by other people. That which you send out will return to you again.

Treat Others with Dignity

A wise man considers his words carefully before he lets them leave the tip of his tongue. Never do, or say, anything to injure or harm another person. Let us treat all people with dignity and respect. After all, all of us are children of our Father in heaven, and not just you and me.

My brother told me a story a while back that I will always remember. He said he was called to a friend's home because her father had passed away. The paramedics were there when he arrived, and he found that this senior citizen who was now deceased, was near his shower, but was still left without clothing to cover him. My brother told me he immediately said to the paramedics, "Come on men, let's give this man his dignity, put some clothes on him."

That one story told me more about the heart of my brother than if I had taken time to read his life story.

Sharing Love with Others

While I am talking about my brother I have one more story for you. For decades, my brother and his wife have been playing Santa Claus and Santa's helper for five or more different faiths and several schools including: pre-schools, kindergarten, up to the fourth grade, every Christmas.

Santa brings a big sack full of presents for the children each Christmas and Santa's helper assists each of the children waiting in line to take their turn to sit on Santa's lap, be photographed with Santa, and tell him all about what they would like for Christmas. This has gone on long enough that the two have seen many of these children grow up to be young men and women.

When I was home for a visit last Christmas, more than one mother brought her children over to my brother's home to let her children sit on Santa's lap and be photographed in front of Santa's Christmas tree with Santa's helper, and the children loved it!

Jesus taught all those who would love and follow him: "Ye are the salt of the earth but if the salt have lost his savor; wherewith shall it be salted? It is thenceforth good for nothing, but to be cast out, and to be trodden under foot of men" (Matthew 5:13).

How is your salt holding up folks? For a man's salt to have any savor and work, a man has to be actually doing something, and if he is, he may as well be doing something good. If you do good and kind acts, your salt will not only be holding up and work, but your life will also have a little "extra taste" in the eyes of others.

Jesus added these words: "Ye are the light of the world. A city that is set on a hill cannot be hid. Neither do men light a candle, and put it under a bushel, but on a candlestick, and it giveth light unto all that are in the house. Let your light so shine before men, that they may see your good works, and glorify your Father which is in heaven" (Matthew 5: 14-16).

Loving God's Children By Helping Them

A friend of mine goes to Kenya every year with his wife, and joins others to dig wells and build schools. Another friend travels to Honduras each spring with a team of doctors to help with needs of the locals in dentistry and facial reconstruction.

Another friend coaches a group of boys the age of his two sons once each week during football season. It was pleasing to see his wife and other family members giving added support and cheering for the boys when they scored a touchdown or made a great play.

I can remember driving across Nevada years ago on my way back to Utah from a visit to

California. I remember driving past a cowgirl broken down on the side of the freeway. I had not seen another vehicle on the interstate for the past twenty minutes. I pulled my car off to the side of the road, put it in reverse and backed up toward her pickup truck. She was towing a cattle car filled with live cattle. The right rear tire of the cattle car had blown out. There was no way she could have taken the bad tire and wheel off and replaced it with her spare tire by herself. I managed to get the bad tire off just fine but when I tried getting the new tire on, I quickly discovered that the weight of the cattle that filled up the cattle car made that task almost impossible. The jack needed to still go up higher by several inches. I tried with all my might and strength to move the jack higher by myself but I could only manage to make it move up two more clicks. I finally had the idea of having the cowgirl climb up on my shoulders. It was only by the combined weight of the two of us that I managed to move the jack up the two extra inches it needed to go to let the new wheel match up with the hub to allow me to cinch up the lug nuts.

    I do not remember being thanked, although I am sure she probably did thank me. That did not matter at the time. I do remember the look on her face for having been rescued and being able to get her cattle to wherever it was she was going, and that was thanks enough.

Another friend once traveled with the USO, entertaining U.S. servicemen and women by bringing them a little hometown cheer. She managed to find me when I was a serviceman in Southeast Asia and we visited the wounded in hospitals together and following her concert for the troops that evening, we were invited to have a nice dinner with the Navy brass.

One of my neighbors and friends told me he was letting a college student, from a nearby state with whom his son had a clerical relationship, stay in his basement for six weeks because he could not find housing. That young man would then be serving others in a religious context in Georgia for two years before returning to finish college.

This friend had also decided to spend an entire day helping and getting to know others better. He began the day by interacting with someone he did not know while doing his grocery shopping. He then took a berry pie and chicken to a neighbor.

 He first found out what kind of pie she preferred. Then he drove another neighbor to where he could purchase a remote device for his hearing aid. I joined him in the evening, and we had fun escorting our 91 year-old-neighbor to one of his favorite eating places, where we all enjoyed dinner together.

That Old Thorn in the Side Called, "The Other Fella's Pride."

It always seems to be the other "fella" who gets accused of having the weaknesses that most all of us have. The only trouble is, when we focus on the other fella's weaknesses, we almost always overlook the fact that we also have at least a smattering of that old thing called pride, ourselves.

Don't be too full of yourself. I can still remember my mother calling me, "little King Tut" once, and only once, in my life when I was about eleven years old. I was probably bragging about being the big leader of all the cowboys and Indians in our neighborhood since I was the oldest. I do not remember what I may have said or done to have my sweet mother call me that. But I still haven't forgotten. I hope I have left the "little King Tut" syndrome far behind me by now.

Ronnie and the Rotations

When I was nineteen, I started my first "Rock N Roll" Band. I named the band, "Ronnie and The Rotations." We played the Holiday Inn in Sacramento, the day before the big dance and show we would be performing on the following Saturday night. The local radio station was there to record our song and to do an interview with us to promote our big dance and show.

A nice lady from the radio station interviewed me when we finished. When the interview ended, we all walked over to the coffee shop and ordered some sodas. Soon, a recording star I recognized sat right next to me, in the coffee shop.

I said hello, then I said, "you are Ray Peterson, I love your hit record, "Tell Laura I Love Her." Then I asked him, if we sounded all right to him. When he said he liked us, I thought, wow, a real live recording artist, Ray Peterson, with a current hit record, likes us.

I thanked him, then he invited all of us to be his guests watching him perform his hit record, and to also watch the starring act, the Righteous Brothers, back stage at the Sacramento Memorial Auditorium on that very night. Were we ever excited!

We all showed up before the show began and the stage manager actually knew we were coming. Imagine that! The stage manager let us back stage. That was pretty big stuff for a teenager back then. When our big dance and concert ended the following night, the band decided to go to Denny's after midnight to celebrate. We were all sitting in a corner booth near the front window. We were all together in our cool signature outfits with our long hair.

Suddenly, four teenage girls walked up to the front window and spotted us. They stopped dead in their tracks and started yelling and screaming, "Ronnie and The Rotations, Ronnie and the Rotations." Then they just began staring at us, as if they were in a trance.

We were all caught off guard. I could feel everything change then. It was as if the stars in the midnight sky were saying, "Ready or not, you are famous now! I'm afraid I may have let that idea go to my head at some point after that happened.

In fact, once I started to believe I really was cool and famous and might soon have hit records on the radio, my head swelled up to the size of one very large melon. If pride can be compared to hot air, my head was filled with enough of it back then that all I would have needed, was a gentle nudge skyward and I may have floated up to the moon.

A False Sense of Importance

I once heard one fella say, "When I leave, they won't be able to get along without me. No one will be able to do the job as well as I did."

Here's a news flash for you, Captain Fantastic: "When you leave, they will get along just fine without you and they may even get along better when someone else arrives with fresh ideas and a new perspective."

Don't Be a Jaw Flapper

Do not be a Jaw Flapper! Think how much more pleasing and beneficial it always is for a listener to hear someone other than "you" tell how many good things "you" have done than for you to flap your jaw about yourself.

When someone else says something nice or complimentary about you when you are present and gathered with others, it will always feel so much better to the listener than if you tell everyone about all the good things you have done.

From the author of Proverbs we are taught: "Let another praise thee, and not thine own mouth; a stranger, and not thine own lips" (Proverbs 27:2).

Self Esteem

Stop looking down. Look up. Hold your head up. Look the other fella square in the eye and hold that look. You are a child of God. Do not be intimidated by another person, not even for a minute. Do not fear another person. Fear God, and honor God by keeping God's commandments and loving all of God's children.

The bully who intimidates with his might, and the poor soul who calls others "worthless," should be pitied and not feared. Even when the intimidator succeeds, they still have only temporary and fleeting self-respect, self-esteem or dignity, because they will always be looking over their shoulder for someone else to come along who will intimidate them.

If you were a prisoner of war, though you may have had to endure torture and the most cruel treatment, your captors could never take your self respect, self worth, self esteem and dignity from you unless you surrender your will to them. Your captors may have you held as a prisoner against your will. They may think they have taken away your freedom. But in reality, no one else owns your will or your freedom.

God gave you your will and your ability to choose. God gave you your freedom, and no man can have that. When you are ready to surrender your will, give your will to God and he will bless you in this life and in the world to come.

I have noticed that when people retire, if they have nothing to do but sit on an easy chair and rock their life away, their life usually ends in a few years. But, when retired people catch hold of the idea that their life still has value, purpose and meaning and that they can still make a valued contribution to humanity, their lives go on and they seem to live to a ripe old age.

Why is that so do you suppose? I believe it is because everyone needs to know they are needed, and when a person gains this knowledge, life takes on a brand new meaning! Self-esteem is something we all need. We all need validation from time to time. It is always nice when someone tells you what you are doing with your life has value and worth. Creative people especially need to have feedback from time to time.

All of God's children need to know they matter. All need to know they are important and that they can make a difference, that our life has meaning and purpose, and that we are not just aimlessly living out our lives without rhyme or reason. Here is "validation," that your life has meaning. You are a child of God. God loves you. God loves you the way you are. God will always love you, no matter what!

Morality

If you want to have success in loving all of God's children, you first must love yourself and respect yourself and that means you must be clean and pure.

"Who shall ascend into the hill of the Lord? Or who shall stand in his holy place? He that hath clean hands and a pure heart" (Psalms 24: 3-4).

Ladies and gentlemen of all ages should dress modestly. In the old west, if a cowboy could see a ladies ankle, the townsfolk would protest that to be immodest. When I was in high school, the young women in the Miss America beauty pageant wore full piece bathing suits. It was the same with the young girls in my high school.

The old TV shows would always show two twin beds when they cut to a bedroom scene. Even Hollywood seemed to be content with innuendo only in at least some of the old movies.

Popularity Vs. Morality

To be popular is a wonderful thing but if being popular means dressing immodestly or doing those things you know you should not be doing, it is not worth the trade. Why? Because being popular for the wrong reasons, and using immodesty to accomplish popularity, will leave a scar on your character. Let your integrity, your honor and your character always be like a precious diamonds to you, and not compromised at any price.

Popularity, fame and fortune are good things if they are accomplished with integrity. But even then, those things can be temporary. The Prophet Job went through an endless array of tests, buffetings and insults from even his closest friends. God tested Job and Job maintained his integrity. He said: "till I die I will not remove mine integrity from me" (Job 27:5).

And because Job kept his integrity, we still remember him today. Keep your integrity.

Many celebrities, politicians, and others of note have attained their fair share of fame, fortune and power but because of sexual indiscretions, they are eventually found out and in a season, their fame and fortune vanish and they are all but forgotten.

The apostle Paul taught the Corinthians: "Know ye not that your body is the temple of the Holy Ghost which is in you" (1 Corinthians 6:19)?

These days, so called celebrities of all ages display their *temples* for all, the world. Hollywood has endorsed immorality, fornication and adultery as acceptable behavior for all.

Jesus warned: "Ye have heard that it was said by them of old time, Thou shalt not commit adultery: But I say unto you, that whosever looketh on a woman to lust after her hath committed adultery with her already in his heart" (Matthew 5:27-28).

Keep Your Morality

Keep your integrity. Keep your morality at all cost. You know what is right and you know what is wrong. If your conscience tells you that you have made a mistake, ask for God's forgiveness and when possible, go to the person you may have offended. If you have made a mistake, repent of your mistake. Repentance is not scary; it is easy.

From Proverbs we read: "He that covereth his sins shall not prosper: but whoso confesseth and forsaketh them shall have mercy" (Proverbs 28:13). What should we do when someone confesses and forsakes his or her sins? Should we condemn them? Should we still treat them like a sinner? Do we try stoning them as those who lived at the time of the adulteress (in the Bible) tried to stone her?

You will remember Jesus saved the adulteress by telling her accusers: "He that is without sin among you, let him first cast a stone at her" (John 8:7). Then the Savior asked the adulteress to look up to see if any of her accusers remained.

When Jesus saw none but the woman remained, he asked, her, 'where are those thine accusers? hath no man condemened thee?" (John 8:10). She said, "No man, Lord" And Jesus said unto her, "Neither do I condemn thee: go, and sin no more." (John 8:11). That is the message, that is the sermon, and those are the operative words of truth to all of us: "Go, and sin no more" (John 8:11).

When a person repents of his sins, God forgives that person. Paul wrote to the Hebrews explaining what the Son of God would do for them if they would repent: "For I will forgive their iniquities and remember their sins no more" (Hebrews 8:12).

You can always love others. You can always help others and lift others up. We have the poor ever with us. Jesus said: "For ye have the poor always with you; but me ye have not always with you" (Matthew 26:11). So if you will get yourself right with God, and get yourself clean and pure, then you will be able to have unlimited success in loving and helping others.

Then God will be able to support you in all the good that you try to do. "Who will ascend to the hill of the Lord and who will stand in his holy place? He that hath clean hands, and a pure heart" (Psalms 24:3-4).

Being Ladies and Gentlemen

Recently, a friend and I were able to see more than a dozen high school couples walking into the same restaurant we were visiting one evening. The young men around 17 or 18 were wearing tuxedos and the young girls were wearing prom dresses. Each young man helped his date to be seated.

Each young girl was wearing a corsage. When we were leaving the restaurant, we noticed the young men opening car doors for the young girls. That was fun to see, but good table manners and being polite alone are not enough to make a lady or, a gentlemen. A little more is still needed. For example: ladies and gentlemen do not tell lies, not even little white lies.

Things Ladies and Gentlemen Should Not Do

Ladies and gentlemen do not gossip, they do not start rumors. Ladies and gentlemen do not say anything bad about another person. A true lady or a true gentlemen would never say or do anything to damage the reputation or character of another person. They are loyal and trustworthy. They can be trusted with your confidences. A gentleman will protect and defend, a ladies honor. It should be the same for a lady. Also, when a lady or a gentleman says they will do something, they do it.

Things Ladies and Gentlemen Should Do

Ladies and gentlemen maintain their codes of honor and integrity. Ladies and gentlemen are kind and considerate. They are always thinking about the other person's comfort and welfare. Ladies and gentlemen display good manners. Ladies and gentlemen are polite and respectful. A lady or a gentleman will always try to make the other person feel as comfortable as possible in every situation. Ladies and gentlemen are considerate of other people's feelings.

Ladies and gentlemen do not take advantage of others because they may have a higher social standing, or more money and power nor because they are a boss or company owner or have more rank than another person.

A gentlemen treats all others with dignity and respect no matter what their rank or station in life may be. It is the same with a lady. A lady or a gentleman does not make others feel they are better than the other person. They do not make others feel they are entitled, and feel that all others must bow and curtsy to them.

How Young Girls Can Be Ladies

I have not yet heard this story told, but I am certain there is a little girl out there somewhere who has a prized collection of Barbie dolls that she holds dear to her heart. There may be another little girl that one day moves into her neighborhood whose parents do not have the means to enable her to purchase or play with even one doll. Her mother may make her a homemade doll and the little girl may love and appreciate the doll her mommy made for her, but secretly she may still wish she had just one Barbie doll of her own.

If the little girl with all the Barbie dolls found out about this and invited the less fortunate little girl to play with her and to be her friend and then offered her as a present, one of her prized Barbie dolls, that little girl who owned all the Barbie dolls would be a lady of the highest order. It is not the treasures of this world that we prize the most that have the ability to truly warm our hearts, but the treasures we hold dearest to our hearts that we give away to the less fortunate. That is what makes a young girl a lady. That is what makes a young man a gentleman.

How Boys Can Be Gentlemen

There is a story about some young boys aged nine to eleven that I have heard told. All of these boys lived in the same neighborhood. They loved the game of baseball, and played baseball all summer long, at the same time, after school. Most of the boys were very good at the game, but one boy, in particular, was the star player. One day, another boy about the same age moved into the neighborhood. He wasn't very athletic, in fact, he was downright clumsy, but he wanted to be a part of the team even though he had never played baseball before.

He was living with his single mother and there was no one to teach him. When the star baseball player discovered this, he went over to the new boys' home, introduced himself and Invited the new boy to be a part of the team. He gave him one of his old baseball gloves, and one of his prized baseball caps. He even purchased a brand new baseball for this new boy, and later on, gave him one of his baseball bats.

When the new boy participated in practice, he wasn't at all good at the game. But, the star player was patient with him and as the weeks of summer passed, the new boy improved, and got progressively better. By the end of summer, he hit his first home run.

What of the boy who helped the new boy to feel like he was a part of the baseball team? That boy was a gentleman. Whatever that boy chose to do later in life, I believe he was headed for a resounding success!

How More Mature Girls Can Be Ladies

There was a girl in her senior year of high school who was diagnosed with cancer just when she was considering running for homecoming queen. She was not a natural beauty, but had many friends, was a lovely girl, and was very kind and friendly. The chemotherapy she was required to take, soon caused her hair to fall out, and she found herself wearing scarfs to school because her family could not afford to buy her a professional hairpiece.

The girl soon began retreating from her friends until they stepped up and took over. Even though two of them were running themselves, they organized a car wash and earned enough money to buy their friend the needed hairpiece. They then even persuaded the owners of a local beauty salon to give their friend a complete makeover.

The girl then decided to muster up her courage and run for queen. Because of the love and support of all of her friends, she won the competition that year. What of her friends and the owners of the beauty salon who stepped up and made her feel as though she too, was still part of her senior class?

All of those involved are ladies, and that quality is much more important than just being popular and voted homecoming queen. To do something for someone else, is always so much more beautiful than to spend all of your time, resources, and energy doing things for yourself.

How Young Boys Can Be Gentlemen

Some time ago now, the mother of one of my friends invited me to lunch with her. She would be taking my friends' two boys, about five and seven, and her stepdaughter about age eight, with her to the Burger King drive-in. I had known all of the children for some time, and I had already given the two little boys some instructions in military discipline.

I told them both it is always the honorable thing to admit you are wrong when you make mistakes and do something you know you shouldn't do. Both of the boys and I had practiced doing ten pushups when they admitted they did something wrong when they were in my care.

Lunch was going well, and everyone was having fun until, without warning, the oldest little boy filled his straw with soda and sprayed it all over the young girl who was his cousin. I stood up and said to the little boy, "come to attention sir. Now, get down and give me ten."

The little boy got down on the ground and counted off ten pushups while everyone around us looked on in a state of wonder. Then I asked him, "Do you have something to say to your cousin?" "I guess so," he said. "Go ahead then," I said. "I'm sorry," he said. "That's the way" I said, "now, let's get back to lunch."

"By the way," I asked. "Did you figure out how to use your straw to spray soda like that all by yourself." "Yep," he said. "That's pretty clever, but let's save that for the swimming pool and let's be sure to only use water." "O.K." he said.

Advice for Girls of All Ages

The following advice for girls of all ages, who would be ladies, comes from my sister: "Do not smack your gum. Also, ladies never eat with their mouths open. Always say, "Please and thank you." Be kind, even if the other person is not kind back to you. Learn how to set the table properly. Do not slurp your food. Be willing to share your toys with others. My sister explained to me that she now knows many successful and wealthy people. One of them just told her, "I can afford to buy my children anything they want, but they are not going to get anything they want."

Get It Done

Should you see something that needs to be done, whether at work or at home, just do it. If you see someone who needs cheering up, a lawn that needs mowing, or someone who needs food or any other kind of help, just do it. Also, remember, if you do kind acts to get something back for yourself, you already have your reward.

If you do kind acts for the fun and love of doing them, your reward will come down from heaven in God's time and in God's judgment and in God's wisdom. Don't think about your reward, rather think about what your next act of kindness will be. Those are the kind of thoughts that will take you to heaven. Those are the kind of thoughts that will allow you to, live with and love all of God's children.

What kind of man does God need today? Answer: a man who is meek and lowly; a man who is humble; a man who is child-like; a man who is teachable, a man without guile. For that kind of man, the angels of heaven will sit up and take notice. Are you that kind of man? Are you that kind of woman?

It isn't easy to live with and love all of God's children. But then it isn't that difficult either. All you have to do is to get started. There will be days when you will make mistakes because we are all human.

Just get back up and try again. When you do, it won't be long until you realize that we can all make a difference. We can all contribute to making our world a better world to live in by ***Living With and Loving All of God's Children.***

Final Thoughts

You can make this a better world by loving all of God's children. All it takes to begin is one small act of kindness. Should you spend your life doing many small acts of kindness, many will attend your funeral.

But for the man who does perform many acts of kindness, and does help others, if he then takes every opportunity to tell the world how good and noble and benevolent he is, and all about, all the good things he has done for so many; the only souls who will attend that man's funeral are family, those who have been paid to attend, or other circling sharks who expect to inherit all the deceased man once possessed.

This story may help you to love God's children: A certain man in his declining years was taken to a rest home to be cared for. When a man of color appeared to help him, he said, "I don't want that (unmentionable words) helping me." We cannot judge him for that, because those were the traditions from which he was raised. But one day, when there was no one else available to help, the man of color did help him and he loved him.

Eventually, the man who needed help asked for this same man to help him. When he was busy, the man who needed help said, "I'll wait for him to help me." The two men began to love one another. They became friends.

When the man who needed care died, the other attended his funeral. He was the only person of color there. Although his job required long hours, and gave him little pay, he took time off to attend his friend's funeral. The surviving man did not even own a suit of clothes. He purchased a suit to honor his friend while attending his funeral.

This is an example of the love of Christ. This is the love that will change a man's heart, give him a new heart and make him a new man in Christ. That love allows all men to become heirs of God and joint heirs with Christ. This is the love that can make a grown man cry. Please experience this love while you are alive.

The End

About the Author

Ronald H. Bartalini was born and raised in California. He has written two books of poetry, *"I Like You Because You Make Me Happy."* and, "Whispers and Sounds." He is also the author of, *"My Greatest Love, Missionary Stories from My Life"* and *"Hoppity Moose and the Red* Caboose." He currently resides in Utah.

Captain's Log

Captain's Log

www.ingramcontent.com/pod-product-compliance
Lightning Source LLC
Chambersburg PA
CBHW060405050426
42449CB00009B/1914